Put on a
Clown Face

Monica Hughes

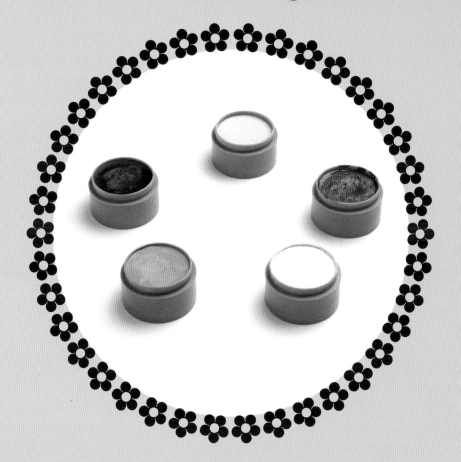

OXFORD
UNIVERSITY PRESS

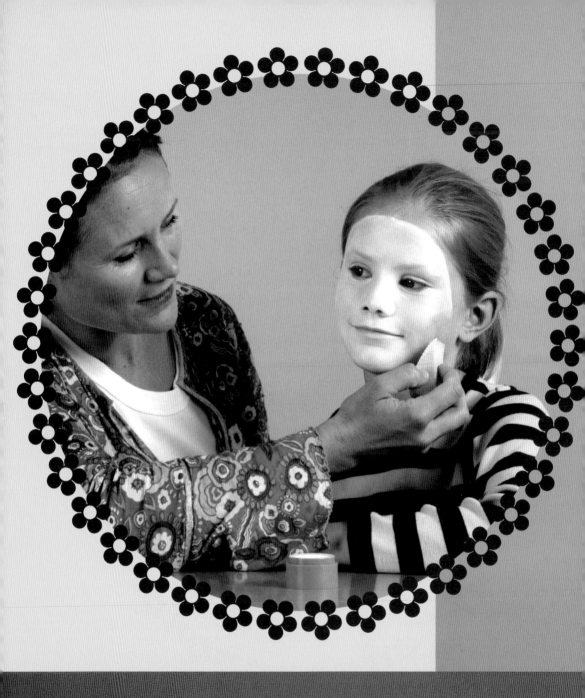

Put on the white face paint.

2

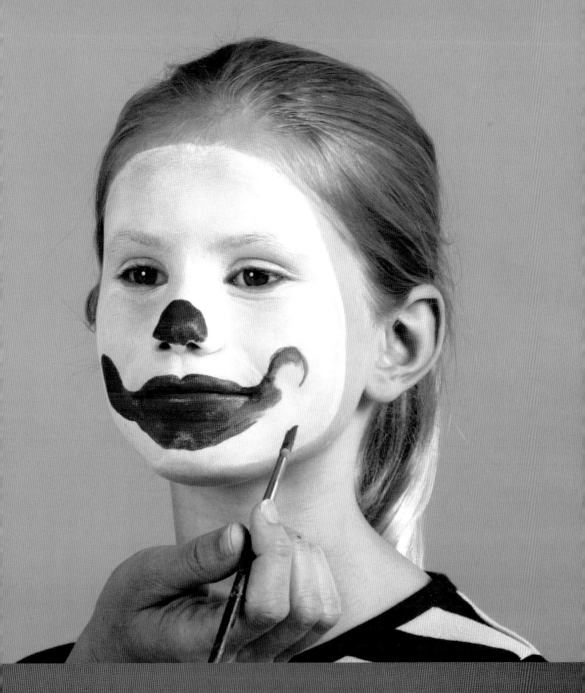

Put on the red face paint.

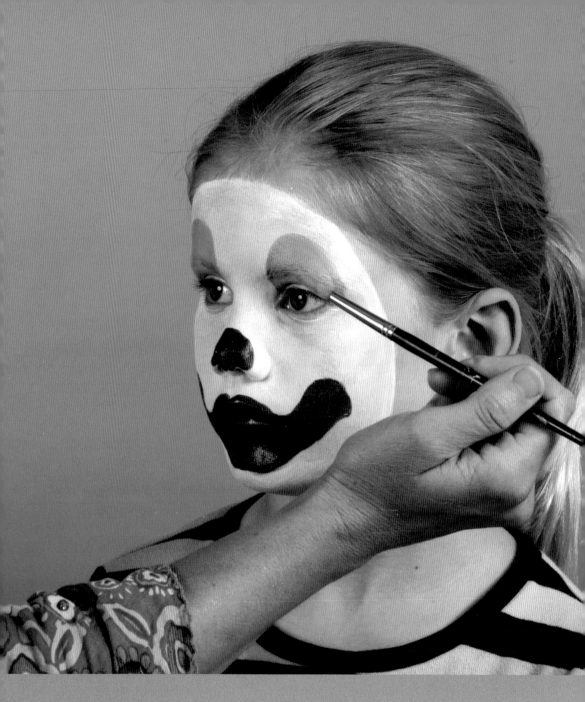

Put on the blue face paint.

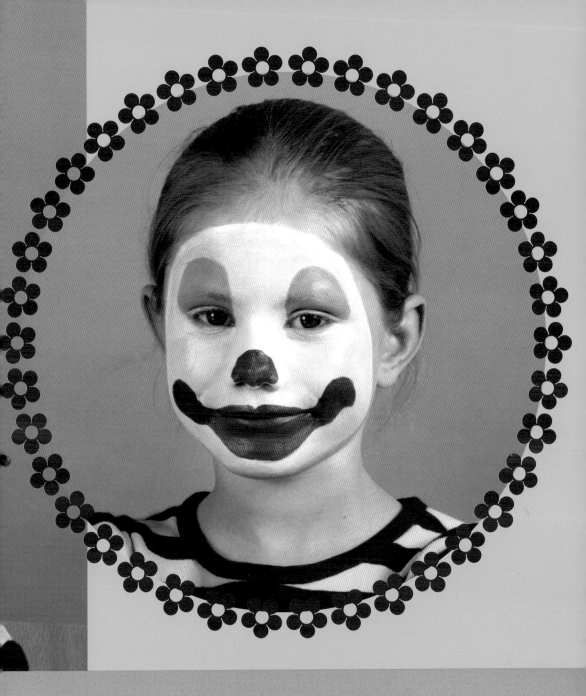

Put on the yellow face paint.

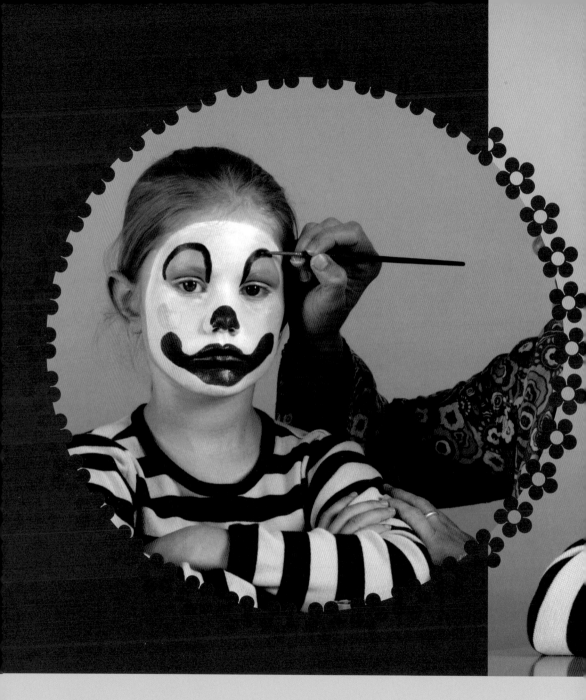

Put on the black face paint.

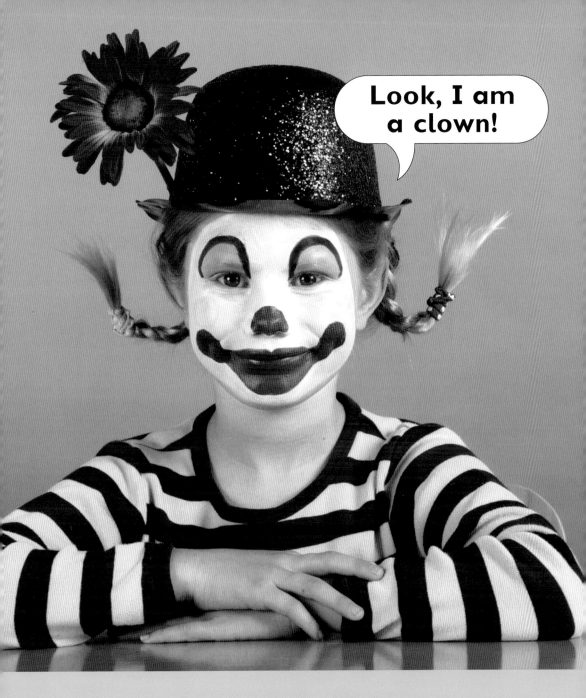

Put on a hat.

A clown face

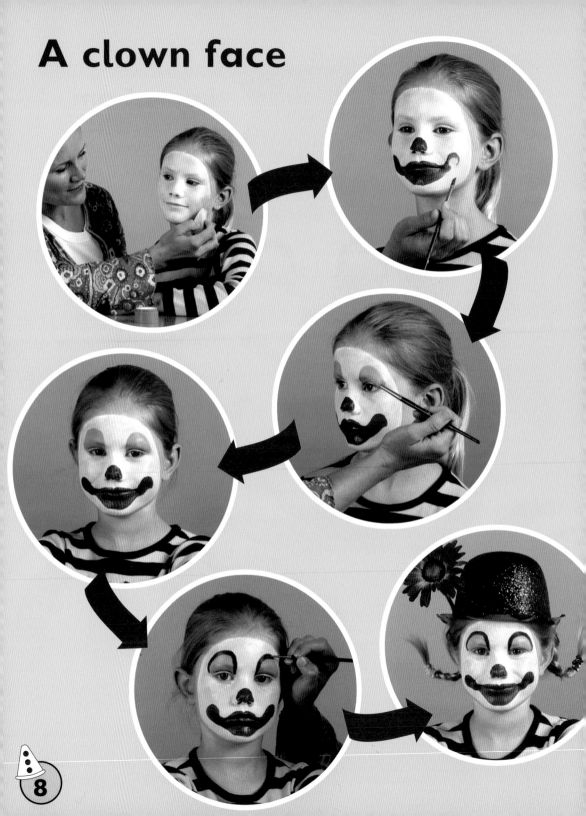